One-Eyed Cat Takes Flight

And Other Poems by

Mitchel Cohen

A Red Balloon Collective
Publication

2008

This book is dedicated to the Memory of
my friends and co-Conspirators

Brad Will

Saralee Hamilton

Susan Blake

Lenny Cohen

Ralph Klaber

Mike Pahios

Will Miller

Enid Dame

Valerie Sheppard

Bryna Eill

Connie Holland

Grandpa Al Lewis

Frieda Zames

Chris Delvecchio, at Highgate

and to Chris Delvecchio, Patty Staib, Kate Berrigan, Shari Nezami, Pat Dalto, Bob Rosado, Gloria Pasin, Fred Friedman, Iris Burlock, Stephen Becker — Comrades, friends, lovers, radicals, fellow poets in the circle in and around the Red Balloon Collective, who died before they could get their full licks in

Rafah, Gaza, March 16, 2003.

(but who at least got in some good ones while they were here); and to Rachel Corrie, Judi Bari and William Kunstler, for standing up for humanity in an era of robots.

Anti-copyright, January 2008

ISBN: 978-1-57027-200-4

**No Borders No Prisons
No Human Being is Illegal**

Red Balloon Collective Books
& the Brooklyn Greens
c/o Mitchel Cohen
2652 Cropsey Avenue, #7H
Brooklyn, NY 11214
mitchelcohen@mindspring.com
www.redballoonbooks.org

Table of Contents

The demand to abandon illusions about our condition is a demand to abandon a condition which requires illusions.

- Karl Marx

Sensitive bugs move   *into Arthur's livingroom*

 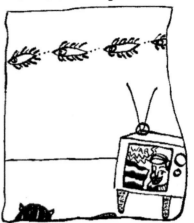

Haideen Anderson

And . . .   *Discover the shocking truth about Arthur & his TV*

THE WASTELAND & ARTHUR THE LION

Shall I sit here sipping my wine
The uncomfortable bald man
Mauled and bewildered?

There is a lion loose in my house.
He stalks the refrigerator, sniffing
The frozen foods,

Huffs at the table, drools on the arugula,
Devours poems by T.S. Eliot (swigging the beer)
And he never brushes his teeth.

On occasion, the lion (whose name is Arthur),
Prowls the terrace, munching
The tomato plants that were my mother's,
Terrifying the gladiola.

When I try to leave the house he stands
On his hind legs and roars
Drooling all over the great purple carpet.
Mollie thinks it's only my friends and she
Contents herself with banging on the wall.
I cannot leave, I am like Zenda, prisoner
Of a poor poetic metaphor.

Recently, Arthur has spent his time
Hogging the bathroom.
He has been practicing a surly sneer
For hours in front of the mirror
To lure Malika into sticking her head in his mouth.

I told him: "Arthur, be reasonable.
Malika's not interested in you.
She likes the Romantic type — you're such a boor."
He asked me to straighten his bandanna.

"Arthur, you're ridiculous.
Get that silly bandanna off your neck."
He sulked around the house all morning, his front paw
Pressed against his head. He burned the bandanna.
He now wears a red beret on top of his mane.

It is hopeless. He won't listen to reason.
He sits around getting more and more grumpy.
At the moment he's in the bedroom making bombs.
"I am an anarchist lion," he bows proudly,
Beret falling to the floor.

All my friends desert me
(I fear Arthur has a homonym in mind!).
"That's an ad hominem attack, to be sure,"
He growls, baring his teeth.
A chunk of hair falls out of his mouth.

"O my god! Arthur, that's not Malika's hair,
Is it?" Arthur says nothing. He sheepishly grins.
"Arthur! Answer me this minute!" I pick up
An ax and chase him to the bathroom.

"Arthur, open up! What have you done with Malika?"
The toilet flushes. A gurgling sound.
I break down the door. Arthur lies
In the bathtub brushing his teeth, his
Spoony eyes in ecstasy. Malika sits there
Rubbing his stomach. "Hullo Daddy-o," she says.

"Malika, what are you doing here?
Are you all right?"
"Of course, silly. I've come to play with Arthur."
Arthur lies there, grinning.
Every once in a while he muffles a yawn.

And so I sit here sipping wine, in my beret,
Soaking up rays
from the television.
Once a week I do the dishes.

I write poems. The last one
Was about Malika. Arthur said
It tasted almost as good
As The Wasteland.

So I've taken to reading poems by others.
The last one went:
"It blows out a mournful sound that swells the sheets
And the beds go sailing toward a port
Where death is waiting, dressed like an Admiral."

Arthur says:
"That's not fair. You can't
Put Neruda's poems in yours."

And what if, so judgmental, his eyes turn to stone
And his body guards the entrance to the Public Library?
We all say things we do not mean
And spend our lives pulling poems, like straws,
From the mouths of broken bottles.

THE BAGEL LADY

The bagel lady gobbles chocolate chips
Between sales. When asked, she gives tips
To strangers on what to eat, the better teas,
And what it takes to please her.

The first time LSD mottled her mind
She peered into a bagel, photographing the world
Through a lens the width of her illusions.
The next few customers pointed:
"That girl!

She's the one. We can tell. She buttered
Our heads incanting mutterations
And stuffed the manicotti
With superfluous musical
improvisations!"

"Ha ha ha, you can't
frame me, there is
No *man*icotti here," she testified
Leaving the stand. She swung her hips
Against the winter of her dreams, slammed

The sexual door on somebody's fingers,
"You're a narc!" she curdled, "But you're
Too late, the evidence is gone, I ate
The last bagel."

UNDERGROUND

Buddha stretches out on the hypotenuse of time.
He has long thin rectangular eyes carved like twin towers

110 floors. A tourist seeks without knowing
To touch someone. The el cuts Brooklyn like a butcher's blade.

After the dentist. Extracting a nerve. Shot novocaine, this heart
Mimics wild horses Cheyenne Wyoming.

He tells it: "Stop. Calm yourself. Take a deep breath. Try
Meditating." He tells himself: "Nazis are after information,

Tell nothing." He is out of control. Promises
Of discipline dribble foolishly in beard.

He sits by the ocean collecting his teeth.
Childhoods on this open beach once romped;

Poems written against these very rocks, there were goats here;
Years ago a teenage girl found him daydreaming, brought him home,

Made him tea, took off his clothing, tumbled into sheets
Too clean for his self-image

And now he comes back, the tourist, gathering roots.
"For tea," he says, tracing his childhood

Down avenues folded up and sealed in his memory
Like a letter written in the heat of passion, O

Where is she? . . . Stuffed into envelope, thrust
Into mailbox 22 cents shy, never received, dead letter

Burning holes in his fingers,
He cannot touch anymore.

Once, he speaks: "Brown rice, beans, cassava,
Café con leché, por favor."

In a corner by a stove a waitress
Works the last two hours of her ten-hour shift

Staring off into space, dreaming
Of another continent without dishes.

He slips a notebook from a side pocket.
"There once was a man with real feelings," he writes,

"And with no price on his soul."
Then he scratches it out. The streetlamp outside turns on.

Waitress counts her tips. In the backdoor of memory
She remembers a song she'd heard as a child

> *Muscrats scamper across the ice —*
> *Top o' the morning, top o' the day —*
> *Left my landlord bound 'n' drunk*
> *In the corner of the ice in an old tin trunk*
> *When the river thaws he'll be swept away*
> *In the middle o' the morning on a mild March day*

Dreams of white horse and rider on the Spanish moor,
Folds her apron, presses button

Elevator down, 110 floors, doors open at last,
She slides like a tear
    out the corner of his eye.

GRADUATION DAY AT PATCHOGUE HEAD START

for Malika, at 5

When the graduates assemble
And each proud and learnèd class
Parades with Pomp and Circumstance
For the last time down the aisle

What a clattering of cameras
And parental hopes amass
For this knot of pristine miscreants
Marching single file

Here comes summer! Freedom!
And the blossoming of youth
The smells of tarry afternoons
Tangled roses and wild children

There goes summer! Autumn
Frowns in someone else's truth,
Conforming into classrooms
Single filing us again.

ON SARTRE'S PUNCTUATION

"Your poems are worse than Hitler."

- George Herbert Walker Bush, preparing to invade
my apartment in Bensonhurst

A point! All I want is a point!
That tiny infinitesimal longing
That rolls undetected through one's gut
Natural selection through the species
Little dots of fiery dreams

Give me a point to hang my hat on
A point to parade all red-faced and huffy
A point to worship, a point to cherish
A silly point, a serious point
A point to dot the i's with
And to punctuate life's sentence

How many points fit in a line?
How many lines in a polemic?
Donald Rumsfeld accentuates his points
By chopping the flat air with the side of his palm
His hot toxic breath
Orders thousands to their death
Point after point
A tower of points, a babel of points
And the points pile ever higher
They are impressive,
irrefutable
So eloquent, convincing us
We all have to die
Right now

Why a point? A comma, give us a comma!
A semi-colon. Anything but a point!
These points are so definitive, like laundry
These points are so teensy little nothings
No length nor width to them
Nothing to measure them by
Pinpricks of emptiness
The hole a bullet leaves
In an Iraqi body, the hole the sorrow leaves
Down the trail of memory

This poem has no points
It races the river's Post-Modern waves
from stone to stone rippling
Its pointlessness proudly!
We sling our words
Like absurd little Davids
Against the Pointagon
A thousand points of fright
Painting the vast canvas of our pointlessness
"Why ya doin' this?"
"What's yer program?"
"Let me see your passport."
"Whaddya hope to accomplish?" —
The utter pointlessness
Of all
Their
Points

THE MACHINERY OF SLEEP TURNS ITS FIRST WHEEL

For Mumia Abu-Jamal, Leonard Peltier, Geronimo Pratt, Susan Rosenberg, Ray Levasseur and, of course, the Zapatistas

> *"Freedom is about authority. Freedom is about the willing-ness of every single human being to cede to lawful authority a great deal of discretion about what you do."*
>
> - Rudolph Giuliani (The Fascist Gun in the East)
> *New York Times, March 17, 1994*

They took the owls
our wolves
our deer

They took our words
and sold
the rain

They took our corn
and coined
the pastures

They took our pictures
and stole
the spirit

They took our forests
and now gasp
for air

They paved our paths
running deserts
corrugated streams

They took our time
the long silence
between heartbeats

They took our shoes
still we are coming
our feet

Wrapped
in the skins
of dreams

CASH-CROPPING EDEN:
NICARAGUA, EXPORT ZONE #7

Matagalpa, Nicaragua (January, 1984)

They work like dogs in a garden of Eden
Plucking red beans into burlap sacks
Lugged at day's end, fingers tender and scratched,
Down the hillside. Grapefruits, green oranges,
Mangoes, and red-meat papayas weigh full,
Juicy but forbidden, as forever
Beyond the campesinos' thirsty reach
As the luscious ripe sun hanging
From the lowest branches. The fruits
Are for export like the coffee, the labor,
Paradise, eyes-only, hands off, unkissed.
First sack is lifted, grunt!, it's tossed
And then the next, heave!, still another
Faster! Faster! Grunts marking rhythm
Sweaty salsa exhaustion, mountains
Pounding their beat against the wood rail.
A snake writhes under shed, keeps it rat-free.
Another sack is heaved, next! next!
To the point-man, enormous arms, straddling
Like a pendulum the pit's edge machête
Cutting cane, slicing the enemy,
Catching the sacks, sweeping the floors —
Dust of history, dust of ancient memory —
Sweep after sweep bronze arms sweep the dusk
Dumping sacks full of beans down the pit's wood throat
Pivots just in time, next fifty pound sack
Thumps the barrel of his chest

Arms surround it and dump, pivot
And dump, catch next sack and dump
Catch it! next sack and dump, next! (grunt)
Next! Next! (grunt) Man sitting on the rail
Logs each peasant's score, Next! Next!
Stub pencil marking sweat-drenched page
Next! Next! (grunt) Pivot and dump
Pivot and dump Merengue and dump
Salsa and dump Clap out those rhythms
New world needs coffee wake up and smell it!
Tumble like musical notes as
Brand new generator — the new Padrone is so proud —
Churns a paddle wheel. Water sloshes through
Its narrow channels, rinses away sprays,
Sweat, the smells of invasion
But still no ventilation fan for the smoke
Thick in the workers' kitchen, where women
Squeeze oranges, heat oil, mash corn.
Cherry red beans tumble in a giant wet heap
Plucked / sacked / counted / dumped / and washed.
Alongside, campesinos stretch out
Drying with beans this last hour of sun.

WHOSE VICTORY? WHOSE DEMOCRACY?

When Jimmy Carter sent Napalm to Somoza

And you, what are you running from,
What secret rendezvous in the crosshairs of history,
What silent rainbow of sadness, of fear?

Here, life crosses the river
And is blown apart
No angel of morning screams for forgiveness.

Chamorro, and Chamorro, and Chamorro
Creep through this bloody war from day to day
To the last contra of recorded Time —
Murderer! Somocista! —
Having militarily lost the war,
Now to be the government enshrined.
All our aspirations had crystalized here
Among these clinics, schools, poet-warriors rising
Against impoverished circumstance
And imperial design. Out, out brief candle!
Life is but a walking shadow, a poor player
That struts and frets his hour upon the stage
And then is voted out. Yankee dollars
Are but half the tale; the other half is *us,*
Revolutionaries by proxy, full of sound and fury,
Signifying nothing.

SAD-EYED COLONELS OF THE LOWLANDS

(to the tune of "The Fox")

Ollie North went down to the House one night
He prayed for Ron to give him light
For he'd many a file to shred that night
Before he left the town-o, town-o, town-o
He'd many a file to shred that night
Before he skipped the town-o.

Fawn Hall found memos of all sorts of deals
Guns for coke and missile sales
"Get rid of'm 'fore we all end in jail!"
Better shred than dead'm, shred'm, shred'm,
Shred'm 'fore we all end in jail
Better shred than dead'm.

Here's one from Secord, one to Bush
One for the yacht and one for the Porsche
Casey'll keep his permanently hushed
But in the meantime better shred'm, shred'm, shred'm,
The old man says he loves my tush
But in the meantime better shred'm.

CIA plane shot down and in distress
Bush met North at his urine test
Said: "Golly, Ollie, another fine mess
I seem to have gotten us into, into, into,"
Said Ollie, "No sweat, I'll just confess
And save your ass and skin, too."

more on nest page

Poor Ollie took it on the chin
For Kukla, Fran and McFarlane
Who took a handful of valium
O all the sad-eyed colonels, gusanos, colonels
I ran Iran and then I ran,
All the sad-eyed colonels.

Now Reagan's term got a new lease —
"Are we men or are we Meese" —
The old fox inked a tax increase
And the contras run the town-o, town-o, town-o
Coke cash rules Washington DeCeased
And the rest of us all can drown-o.

Ollie North went down to the House one night
He prayed for Ron to give him light
For he'd many a file to shred that night
Before he left the town-o, town-o, town-o
He'd many a file to shred that night
Before he skipped the town-o.

Department of Just Desserts: During Ollie North's failed election campaign for U.S. Senate in 1994 Fawn Hall, his former secretary who had lied so brazenly to Congress in the Iran/Contra/Cocaine hearings, entered a rehab facility for cocaine abuse.

THE REAGAN YEARS

"We begin bombing in five minutes."

There once was a mad master baiter
Who lusted the isle of Grenada
He pricked the oasis
with milit'ry bases
And erected himself its dick-tator.

EMULATING MARX

I am becoming more like Marx every day —
My belly is growing, and my beard is turning gray.
I have no money, and while thus far I have been spared
The famed boils on my buttocks I have no doubt
My constipation is but its prelude, and I think about
French pornography, police, the working class and all the weird
Formulaic elegies and witches' brews of dubious distinc-
Tion that Gorbachev et al. are forcing us to drink.
And woe to those who've sold their souls for trinkets,
The thrill of market victory, and the agony of deceit.

I am becoming more like Lenin every day—
Balding, isolated, corpse on display
For new generations to behold and possibly to spit on!
Is nothing sacred? Is there no longer room
To predict the weave of history upon her silent loom?

GLASNOST (in every day life)

Please, in the morning, don't open
the goddamn windows like you do every day.
Not that I mind the fresh air after
a listless night of necromance dreams,
but these routines,
they carve us up, stamp our wrists,
sneeze us out

Please, in the afternoon, don't slam
the goddamn door like you do every day.
Not that I mind you running down
for the mail (we are all lonely)
it's just I hate to be awakened so rudely,
my insomnia you know, only
way to cure it is to
sleep it off

Please, in the evening, don't bang
the goddamn pots like you do every day.
Not that I mind the polemics while cooking
but all this Russian food, & Russian cups
with iron curtain handles clanging again,
this migraine you call "democracy,"
don't remind me, when you bang the pots

LAST TANGO IN GDANSK, or Socialism in One Song

(to the tune of She'll be Comin' Round the Mountain)

It's Lech Walesa's birthday in Gdansk
They have painted red carnations on the tanks
They have shorn no frill or folly, hey!
Made it a national holiday
Those wild and crazy comrades in Gdansk

There'll be orgiastic praise in CP's press
Parading bureaucrats in their Sunday best
Lining up like nuns on acid bummers
Disco to the same old drummers
Snort coke supplied by bankers in the West

The prison gates will open, and no doubt
When they do the real dragons will fly out
They will feast on meat and vodka — yea! —
And play on the harmonica
Punch the stinkin' corpse of Stalin in the snout!

Ain't it neat, and Oh so grand! says Bush,
Not a commie in the land,
Regardless of the figleaves that they wear.
The heroic Internationalé
Bows to CitiBankers' Capitalé
And the working class can kiss their derrière

It's Lech Walesa's birthday in Gdansk (in Gdansk!)
They have painted red carnations on the tanks (thank the pope!)
They have shorn no frill or folly, hey!
Made it a national holiday,
Those wild and crazy comrades in Gdansk.

THE GNAWING OF THE MICE
The Socialist Scholars Conference & Grad School Theses

O where do they find all that time to sink
Into minute review of Marx's life? —
Ev'ry belch and fart, scat inf'rence — I think
Forever could they tender fine distinc-
Tions and forego the living for dead trif-
Les, explore glum trails of contradiction
With dialectical incision
Finely tune the fuzzy mental axis
To camouflage the graveyard their praxis
Details: Every split, bleak feud or faction
To "prove" the futility of action!

O paralysis of analysis
Seductive ivory-tower palaces
Guerrillas of thesis-war protracted
Emerging biographers contracted
In tenure's sterile wonderland, all hail
Your People's Delegate from Bloomingdale's!
Providing gossip, letters, notes — What is the sound
Of one class struggling? — which, when all life dries up, to turn
And thrive in muck no prole need ever learn —
Consume names, dates, debates, their lives affirmed
Till human voices wake them, and
they drown.

THE CAT IN THE SOMBRERO, CONTRARO

Lenin leapt from her arms
& took a bite out of Kautsky

Where's Haideen? he snarled
I miss Haideen, you can

Take your Beethoven & shove it
Kautsky couldn't hear tho

He had a point, knew
What was to be done

And left his April feces
As a present outside the box

For his August master.

GUERRILLA

Not without warning does night patrol.
Get to recognize its step,
The brooding eyebrows of winter.

Not without caution does night connect
The fuse. The crossed wires
Short circuit. The yellow bursts

sing.

SONNET

for Raana

You've left your thumbprints all over my back
Vibrations that heal, palm against wounds
So deep they go unseen, calm against attack
Raising Millennial memories from my body's ruins

And so you splash puddles of loneliness
On your face, beneath your feet, feel
The ghosts of longing lapping at your heels, undress
In darkness, hold a candle by your face, steal

Into the closet for a change of clothing —
A hidden corridor of make-believe and silks —
And back again into the room where I, loathing
The emissaries of deceit, their lashes of guilt

Have hung my soul like laundry in the sun
To be folded by your fingers —
   and then the knots were none

Alternate Title: *Marx, Massaging Hegel's Negations*

MORNING

When first the glint of dawn has reached
A blind hand on the window ledge
And steals into my room, a coin
Upon its palm my bets to hedge

No beggar would I more endure
No lumpen prole is welcomer
I keep a pot of coffee warm
For this most ungrateful burglar.

WITH A KNOCK ON THE DOOR

for Dennis Bernstein, and the Sanctuary Project

So they came for her one morning
It was not a dark and stormy night
The air was crisp and the smell
of tortillas and fried beans
raked the leaves. A newspaper,
unopened, she used to smack
an occasional fly. Up North
a centerfielder tried to catch them.

So that is what it was like, a warm
late summer morning awash
in detail. For the writer
every detail is a prism, is power:
Change from "Mary" to "Malika"
and the constellations whirl,
from "John" to "Romero" and lambs
thunder like wild horses.
What are their names?
Write down their names!

What else do you need, drinking coffee,
reading the papers before going to work?
Why they came? What happened?
And what if it was not sunny?
If there was no smell of beans?
If the electric cattle-prod
they shoved up her vagina
bought with "humanitarian aid"

was 110 volts and not 220?
If *The Times* reported nothing
of the day's actual events? If
the centerfielder missed the ball?

These details — Why do we crave them
in the morning
refrying the news?

HAIKU: CLEARING THE AIR

Zone E: Virginia:
Blackbirds are weeping tarred husks
Turned ice, frozen tears

Army sprayed the trees
Chemical paint black gluey
Pours into the nests

Warning redbirds wail
Lookouts leap from their perches
Screeching endlessly

Talons tear at tar
The clogged feathers, the frantic
Beat of withered wings

Again the sky bursts
Fleeing birds panic, tumbling
In great tarry heaps

Earth, and broken wings
And broken leaves, and the bark
Scraped with desperate beaks

From the bones of trees
And the wind, and the cold tar
Suddenly quiet

Airways cleared at last
Jets and bombers may now sweep
free to foreign wars

Unimpeded by
Anti-imperial birds
El Salvador? Hush.

1492

"[The Arawak] brought us parrots and balls of cotton and spears, which they exchanged for glass beads and hawk's bells. They willingly traded everything they owned. They were well-built, with good bodies and handsome features. They do not bear arms and do not know them, for I showed them a sword, they took it by the edge and cut themselves out of ignorance. They have no iron. Their spears are made of cane. They would make fine servants. with 50 men we could subjugate them all and make them do whatever we want."

- Christopher Columbus, from his Diary, after the Arawak Indians discovered him on their beach

There are nightmares that climb out of bed
without their clothes on. Who knows
where they started? They walk out
on their own, stagger into the street,
they're halfway down the block
before you catch up

They are generally European,
occasionally tall, and always
of food. They remember things
you'd expect they'd have forgotten
a long time ago: the silly masks,
the tunnels at the end of the light,
the gnawing emptiness
you tried to stuff with wine,
with food, with books, and religion
like a Christmas stocking
on a chimney
in the winter
in the snow

But when hunger bites you in the eye
and the washed out faces
roll in with the fog
from Iraq and from Iroquois,
Arawak and Palestine,
South Africa, Somalia,
Panama, the Philippines, Puerto Rico, East Timor,
Haiti and El Salvador, Santo Domingo,
Bosnia, Grenada, the Ukraine
and their words are impossible,
and their pictures
are like photos from Venus,
and you sit there
stuffed with fog
tears refusing to come,
they well up in the behind parts
of the eye and to each tear
you fix a name, a face,
a hunger, there is nothing else;
they roll in with the fog
wave after wave
smashing endlessly, forever,
impossible — those words;
impossible — those pictures,
"No (no!), No (no!), Nothing (nothing!)," the
hunger
rolls in.

The tears roll down the inside hollow of our bodies,
little drops of fiery dreams
eroding the bones of our cheeks,
ghosts dripping.
Stomach's bayonets jab at the tears,
Stealth mouth is thirsty forever
its star-spangled loneliness

never kisses the water — wake up! wake up! —
But this is one nightmare that never ends.
It goes on and on, and it hungers
in the very bottom of existence.

George Herbert Walker Columbus Bush
is blowing off his hot guns
New World Ordering Iraq
missiles bristling at the zipper.
In Germany, Green Joschka Fisher
hungers for missiles
is learning French, J'ai faim, J'ai faim
an "environmental" Green hunger
(German accent notwithstanding)
where to starve is not to die but to
morté — such classical grace —
with the Mona Lisa watching.

But this is an Amerikan hunger
strictly honky starvation
no embellishment, no ritual
uncultured and rotten
a hunger that grips you
in the back of the knees
and hangs you upside down injecting
bubbles of blue emptiness into your veins.
"Consume!" it calls out.
"Nina! Pinta! Santa Maria!"

and the syringe is the size of a lover, O yes!
and the kisses, the fleshy
zipless stained–glass hallucinations
that pass for lovers
are no cure
no cure at all

WHY CHRIS THREW THE CHAIR

for Chris Delvecchio (8/24/69 - 8/9/93)

I yearn to forsake all words
the way they've forsaken me

The intricate windings down cold stone paths;
the creaking of ancient iron gates; the knocking

On oak doors: Bam! Bam! And into the castle
the wordsmith steps, cautious, careful — "Hey!

Ya gotta problem here? Need a vowel?"—
Describing every torchpit, the pools of darkness

That empty into the keeper's eyes, black holes
of loneliness, where the dogs of society howl

Lose all your love, lose all your dreams, lose yourself
Swimming forever in the dungeon of words, whispering

from every cranberry bush, from every mountain top,
always words, and the pure living act destroyed.

I yearn to forsake all words,
so convincing the tales, the wisdom,

The different ways to reconstruct the emptiness,
the debates, the books, the vicarious ink. And yet

I write why I should never write, that I
shall empoem no more forever.

Listen! Can you hear it:
The existential gasp of new words forming!

GIMME THAT OLD TIME RELIGION

For Jerry Fallout & the Moronic Minority

Gimme that old time religion
Gimme that old time religion
Gimme that old time religion
it's good enuf for me

You'd better follow old Jehovah
all the rules the way he's told ya
or our tanks'll run you over
he's good enuf for me

And of course his good son jesus
nothing but his dad's prosthesis
burn the women, bless the fetus
he's good enuf for me

Gimme that old time religion
Gimme that old time religion
Gimme that old time religion
it's good enuf for me

We will worship Zarathustra
and thus spake the way they useta
I'm a Zarathustra booster
he's good enuf for me

And how about that Aphrodite
so supple yet so mighty
prayin' to her in her nightie
that's good enuf for me

Hari Krishna he must laugh on
to see me dressin' up in saffron
with my hair that's only half on
that's good enuf for me

We will bow to tubby Buddha
of the gods there ain't none cuter
comes in silver, brass & pewter
he's good enuf for me

Let's celebrate with sister Isis
always there in every crisis
cured me of the heartbreak of psoriasis
she's good enuf for me

Now let us crusade for Islam's Allah
Mohammad speaks (for just one dollar)
I'm Farrakhan's Allah Scholah
(So what if he helped frame Malcolm X)
he's good enuf for me

That Israeli religion
wants the power of dominion
shootin' down the Palestinians
it's good enuf for me

Jimmy Swaggart is away now
down in Santiago Bay now
sayin' prayers with Pinochet now
it's good enuf for me

Sandino — well, you'll live in heaven,
just drop your AK-47

at the Managua 7-11
the burgers are on me

Sun Myung Moon he's got your mantra
sell the flowers that he wants ya
to send weapons to the contras
it's good enuf for me

They're all dancin' in a circle
all the gods and ev'ry cler'cal
passing wind and circle jerkin'
us off enuf for me

Gimme that old time religion
woman's place is in the kitchen
see you at the Inquisition
it's good enuf for me.

*New Lyrics by Mitchel Cohen, John Saudino,
Judy Gorman-Jacobs. Add your own!*

DIALECTIC

We know the taste of apple
only relative to the tastes
of everything else

The color of sky
only against that
of grass

Everything contains all else
implicitly in defining itself

Nothing exists for our senses
isolated, alone

Still, to know the apple
you must bite it

To know that "to know
the apple you must bite it," you must

have bit *something* before,
if not the apple

The category expands
with the abstraction

I sit here in the rain
getting soaked, thinking

"To know the rain
I must get soaked."

IN THE BLACK HILLS

Climbing into the pines
inconspicuous as berries
in black slate rocks

There is life that goes unseen
first pass-through:

the bird
with the burnt-orange head,
pale yellow neck, black body
wrestling a worm;

the silent fern
fingering loose
flakes of light;

the exact moment of morning;

purple asters
coming distinguishable;

the metallic reflection
of pen's clip
crossing the page.

These I see only on return
when the soaring spirits
the pines and the constant slap
of rapid city creek
recede, no longer dwarf
and evaporate

the molecules of laughter
the furious details

Free the piney spirits *in* us
blurred gradations
of color and chaos
the invisible web
we suck
into our lungs
exhaling history
moisture
the slow damp eruption
of detail

gasping
like berries
in the mouth
of forgiveness

POEM FOR THE ELECTION YEAR:
IF EDGAR ALLAN POE ATE AT McDONALDS, or
"WHERE'S THE BEEF?"

Once upon a noon-tide hour
As I munched a quarter-pounder
Pondering after glimpses
Of window'd burgers broiled
Suddenly there came a throbbing
Hydrochloric violent mobbing
McCain and Clinton, nuclear lobbing
Burgers at my stomach walls
"Only nausea, Nothing more."

O how painfully I remember
How I retched straight through November
Election Day left me dismembered
Voiceless, bankrupt, violent tempered
Heaving after choice pretended
Lost behind that curtained door —
McDonald's or Burger King? —
When suddenly, without fair warning
I found my battered bod ignoring
Civic pride, decorum, all the drawings
Of "democratic" zeal, disgorging
Vomit on the list of corporate whores —
Quarter-pounders, Nevermore.

ALIVE AGAIN!

*"If I can't revolt,
I don't want part of your dance."*

— with apologies to Emma Goldman

Here comes Autumn
kicking off her heels
letting loose
the wild spirit in her
whip   snap
knees jigging out
a most Kwanza beat
and the blue,
that great crisp democratic
bluster of a skirt
rustles, dips
and swirls up all around her.

My, that Autumn
with the cheeky roses,
1930s radio voice,
cotton-crued sweater,
dances up a storm!
The teary olive-drab smudges —
late-summer horse-breathed romance;
muggy, genital, bayonetal heat;
colorless tar, sticky cities of tar —
leap to attention in neat
pixelated rows and salute!
Laughter spills
like marbles

from an old cheesecloth sack
"dink.
Dink dink dinkdinkdinkdink."
The hats come out and blow off —
These are showerless days
and radiant nights.

Somewhere October
curls up under the quilts —
This then, this then is life! —
"Let me reacquaint you
with my body" Autumn sings
curling her tongue
up the thighs of revolt.
O, all those
vast and noble reasons to live!
those untamed tangos
holy sap of her maples;
sunbeams jigging an Irish echo
in her sycamores and elm;
the deep-throated cussing;
the kicking-out the jams! O,
that Autumn, she can dance!

NOT SOWETO, IN AUTUMN

They painted a bloodred moon on a black canvas
And hoisted it over Soweto.
Not a drop bled into the plaster.
Only the lightning cast the bones of September
Like I Ching sticks against horizon
With its sizzling ozone, uncertain aroma.

Who will claim such misbegotten art?
Who will wear the lightning in her hair?
Biko broods, chained to his dungeon cell:
"Don't look back even once you'll be
Trapped forever here." That old goat Winter
Cackles in his cotton beard.

Persephone by candlelight.
A room in New York City.
Contemptuously the clock hurls its moments
Like bolts into the silence,
Pre-fab banners unintentionally vapid.
The first snows of loneliness batter the fireplace
Sticks ablaze with memories
Of Soweto's autumn tears.

A shirt unbuttons
A radio clicks off against the stars
A hand inadvertently brushes a tear,
a cheek. Icicles burn in her eyes.
Fire-engines scream in her fingers.

In what quarter of night did Jesus anoint

These special search patrols with
Such blisters of privilege, flickering
Textures of ancestral memory?

She rants in Russian.
The light burns a sickle in the ceiling
Scything portraits she had memorized,
Painted, bloodred moon, black canvas
Once-upon-a-time
Not Soweto, in Autumn.

SAFETY FIRST! BE SURE TO WEAR A CONDOM WHEN YOU'RE SHOOTING UP

Stay home they said
don't go to the demo on Saturday
it's too cold
You'll go to jail
You'll miss "24"
and never know
what new inventive ways
Kiefer Sutherland will torture
his latest enemy
and save the world

Stay home they said
there's ice everywhere
nothing is working
Y2K
stay home
watch TV
how cold it is outside
everyone, all together now:
stay home

Stay home they said
don't walk
your goldfish
E.Coli are frozen
in the trees
Even the Malathion
is cracking off
air is crystal clear

lungs not used to it
you will die
unless you
stay home

Stay home they said
it's very very windy
wind chill factor
is minus 5,000 degrees
oooooh
sun too bright
will bounce the ice
jiggle memories
will
upset you

Stay home they said
watch tv golf
from Vega Baja
don't go out to read
your poems, metaphors
will stick in your teeth
and break off
like stalagmites
and it will be
very
very
painful
'sides
your poems are really
not that good anyway
and you can't afford

the dentist
and you can't afford
the movies
and you can't afford
to be arrested
42,000 cops
on prowl today
gunnin' for terrorists
you may be one
even if you're not
from Afghanistan
and there's nowhere
to throw away garbage
(bombs in the garbage cans)
and there's nowhere
to mail a letter
(bombs in the mailboxes)
and there's nowhere
to go to the toilet —
(bombs in the plumbing)
especially do not take the train
traffic lights
are stuck
green
huge chunks of ice
are falling
from Manhattan Bridge
Science Report: Cold contracts
tracks
may collapse
you will certainly plunge

into East River which
is very
very
cold
and no one
will
help
you

Stay home they said
lock windows
duck tape'm
(Quack!)
don't look out
you will turn into
a pillar of ice
stay home
read the calendar
between commercials
don't let nature touchya
don't let **anyone** touchya
You might
get Smallpox
You might
get mugged
You might
get SARS
You might
get West Nile
Anthrax
Avian Flu

Stay home
wait
till we tell you
it is safe
secure
Stay home
check your e-mail
fold the flag
watch TV

ONE-EYED CAT TAKES FLIGHT

A Lullaby

The cat leapt out of the tree last night
Through the air like a red balloon
While everyone slept in beds tucked tight
We rode by the light of the moon

With a "Yip, Yippie!" you grabbed the reins
Silk and scarlet lacing
Faster than the aeroplanes
Through the sky a-racing

We passed over lands where children laugh
And the heavens filled with birds
On the back of the cat you took a bath
And taught me many words

We soared over countries where men make war
And fight with guns and rocket
Rounded them up, threw them 'way on a star
Froze it, chained it, locked it

From way up high down to the street
We poured lots of honey
So people would have enough to eat
And never again need money

Around and around the world we flew
Over China, then Egypt, then Spain
Then quick as a cat, we're back before anyone knew
And tonight we'll do it again.

SAY THE RIGHT THING

I want to write the poem that moves
the conscience of the world
but my words won't leap off the page
the way I'd like, powerfully built,
compact, knocking the universe
for a loop, beating their tender fists
against the stars. They plod
in clanky armor, pedestrians in the city.
Velcro sidewalks snarl
feet stuck in tar —
Who turned up the gravity?
The people
united
will never be
de-feeted (oh!) —
Run, dammit, run!
My poems yearn to skinny-dip **sans serif**
(leave those tiny feet behind)
have to stop every few minutes
to sop their faces
with orange bandannas.
They get diverted by toothaches,
posters (always studying the font),
the endless series of meetings that can't be missed,
the fear of going naked,
the humor in biting an apple,
the steam spraying Broadway from open manholes,
the stench of poverty stumbling towards them from the bars.
My words have nothing new to say about sex

and so avoid it. Sex is a misdemeanor,
the more I miss de meaner they get.
Groan. See, I told ya. My words
take 3 pages when Orwell's take one,
go on unexpected vacations
go on strike inside my pen
smudge ink all over their faces
are becoming vegetarians
clamor: Free Mumia Abu-Jamal!
Free Leonard Peltier! but, by themselves can't & know it.
Lunch hour: they slip
into underground newspapers, hope for a miracle —
what else could they do? —
before trudging didactically
back to the office
for their afternoon shift.

AMONG THE REDWOODS

for Judi Bari

Hello old friends, it's been many years
Ere I walked among ye, towering

Duffy mulch absorbs each step
Woods burl with life emerging

Here, warless warriors born before the Crusades
Bear regal witness to the graceless masquerade

Of new and newer holocausts. Omipotent hum
Of chains saw your wisdom

Establish greed's dominion
Profits über alles; Let me touch your skin

And not possess it, kiss your ancient lips, spill
My memories skyborne into your arms

Hear your silence slap the buzzing air
Fingers blazing with contempt

And join your final stand. At last
To soar among ye, towering.

SONG FOR BRAD WILL (1970 – 2006)

More than anything in this world
I want peace to blossom
More than anything in this world
I want love to flow
More than anything in this world
I want freedom to ring out
Write me a long letter
Tell me how hopeful you are
Roll me a sonnet
Another hit of life

More than anything in this world
I want to know you like a river
More than anything in this world
I want our streams to flow together
More than anything in this world
I want to sail upon those waters
Write me a long letter
Tell me how hopeful you are
Roll me a sonnet
Another hit of life

NINTENDO WARS

I stand and look out
soldier in a tower
silently the hours
spill onto the sands
silently the night leaks
image of a leader speaks
in every home, such power
in every dream, such power
I stand and look out
soldier in a tower
silently the hours
bleed into these sands

THE HITCH-HIKER

The first girl I knew
wore her hair down to her shoe
holes in the bottom

I wonder how she will wear her hair:
Twisted in braid?
Cropped like a ticklish monk?

Forty years ago she kissed me
under the stairwell in her dorm at Stony Brook
hands nibbling
the outskirts of my trousers
eyes surveying the creases
like the captain of a ferryboat
on the Long Island Sound

Three years later she left me
to chase anarchists under beds. Dreams
which flooded our room
on muggy days in July
froze up in the Sound
like ducks caught
in the quick winter ice

Forty years later she writes:
"My dearest delicious Mitchel, won't you
curl your tongue into my crack
I am longing, horny, lonesome
and you've forgotten me"

The sky is starless

like a pocket with no change in it
no clinking in the far off galaxies
and the black highway pavement is soaked

ABOUT THE AUTHOR

Photo by Laura Troup

Mitchel Cohen lives in "The People's Republic of Brooklyn" and makes his living (such as it is) selling his poems in the subways. He was a founder of the Red Balloon Collective and poetry "conspiracy" at SUNY Stony Brook in 1969, was one of the "Liberty Bell 7" arrested for demanding freedom for political prisoners Mumia Abu-Jamal and Leonard Peltier, and co-founded Recycle This!, the No Spray Coalition (www.nospray.org), and NY State Against Genetic Engineering. Mitchel serves on the Local Station Board of WBAI radio (99.5 FM), co-edits "G", the newspaper of the NY State Greens/Green Party of New York, and hosts a weekly radio show, "Steal This Radio," heard via the internet at TribecaRadio.net.

Other works by Mitchel Cohen include

- *The Permanent Carnival* (Selected Poems, 2006)

- *Zen-Marxism: Subjective Factors in Devising Revolutionary Strategy* (printed as a series of 17 pamphlets – includes the classics *What Is Direct Action?, How to Spot a Vanguardist at 20 Yards, Those Not Busy Being Born Are Busy Dying,* and *Fear and the Art of Neurosis Maintenance*)

- *I Was A Teenage Communist* (memoirs, printed chapter-by-chapter as a series of pamphlets)

- *Read My Apocalypse: Notes on the Gulf War*

- *The Capitalist Infesto (Notes on the Ecological Dimension)*

and numerous topical, political and environmental essays

available from

**Red Balloon Collective
c/o Mitchel Cohen
2652 Cropsey Avenue, #7H
Brooklyn, NY 11214
mitchelcohen@mindspring.com
www.redballoonbooks.org**

REMEMBER BRAD WILL 1970 - 2006

Brad Will was my friend, comrade, and independent journalist who went to Oaxaca, Mexico to cover the working class uprising there. His daily video and print reports appeared on IndyMedia websites throughout the world and galvanized support for the Oaxaca communards. Brad — always eyes a-twinklin' — signed his messages "B-Rad". As one writer observed, Brad was "a freight-hopping, guitar-playing activist, who had spent years on the frontlines of countless movements from efforts to save squats and community gardens in NYC's Lower East Side to engaging in 'tree-sits' for weeks at a time high in the canopy of Oregon's endangered old-growth forests." He took part in the landless struggle in Brazil and traveled throughout the Americas documenting struggles against the forces of capitalist global-

ization. Brad was assassinated in Oaxaca on October 27, 2006 by death squads affiliated with the Mexican police, funded in part by the U.S. government. Although there are a number of photos of the perpetrators, the assassins have been released from custody. This book is dedicated to my friend Brad Will, and the dreams he inspired and lived for.

Photo of Brad Will, from BradWill.org